CONTENTS

BOMBPROOFING
TIPS

4   Introduction
5   Understanding the horse's nature
6   Basic riding skills
8   Leading skills
10   How to de-sensitise your horse
12   Riding past objects of fear
14   Traffic, tractors, bikes, horses and carts, etc.
16   Loud noises and unusual sounds
17   Reward and punishment
18   Riding over objects on the ground
20   Animals and children
22   'Strange' objects
24   Conclusion

INTRODUCTION

Horses are timid creatures and it is natural for them to be afraid of things that are unfamiliar to them. Of course, it is not ideal for us to ride a horse that is nervous and reacts to everything in our path, so we have to get him used to anything and everything that we may encounter when out riding, and teach him that the world is a safe place. The common term for a horse that accepts everything without being afraid is 'bombproof', implying that even if a bomb went off nearby, the horse would not react, jump sideways or try to run away.

Horses are amazing animals in that they will accept just about anything once they are used to it: look at what horses have done in times of war, what police horses are trained to do and the kind of things that horses will do in movies. What all of those horses have in common is that somebody has taken the time to train them to be bombproof – and

this is something that practically any horse can be trained to be, including yours and mine.

Of course, we can never predict what unexpected things we may encounter when we are out riding, but there are lots of things we can do to make the unexpected happenings safer and easier to manage: basic schooling of the horse, an understanding of the aids by both horse and rider, and the rider being relaxed and developing a good, quiet seat, can help immensely. Developing a partnership, a trusting relationship between horse and rider, also plays a valuable part in having a bombproof horse, as well as taking the time to teach the horse to be calm, by exposing him to all manner of potentially frightening objects in a safe place, such as a riding arena, where he can have the time he needs to look and discover for himself that he is safe.

BOMBPROOFING TIPS

by
Perry Wood

Illustrations by
Carole Vincer

KENILWORTH PRESS

Copyright © 2005 the Kenilworth Press

First published in the UK in 2005
by Kenilworth Press, an imprint of Quiller Publishing Ltd

Reprinted 2010, 2013, 2014, 2015

British Library Cataloguing-in-Publication Data
A catalogue record for this book
is available from the British Library

ISBN 978 1 872119 88 5

Printed in China

Kenilworth Press

An imprint of Quiller Publishing Ltd
Wykey House, Wykey, Shrewsbury, SY4 1JA
Tel: 01939 261616 Fax: 01939 261606
E-mail: info@quillerbooks.com
Website: www.kenilworthpress.co.uk

UNDERSTANDING THE HORSE'S NATURE

It can be tempting to think that your horse is stupid or that he is 'playing up' when he is afraid of something that we know to be safe, but actually, a horse showing this instinctive behaviour is far from stupid – in fact, as far as the nature of horses is concerned, he is being sensible.

Because horses are prey animals they are afraid or suspicious of anything new. In the wild, prey animals that are not alert enough to run away from danger can be killed and eaten by predators. Domestic horses retain this instinct and still think in this way.

It is important to recognise, though, that every horse is different, so while one horse will be afraid of certain objects, another will not be bothered by them at all.

Interestingly, horses have two quite separate halves to their brain – left and right – and research has shown that the two sides don't talk to each other very much. This may explain why your horse can be perfectly happy about an object by the roadside as you ride out, but then shies at it, as though he has never seen it before, when you ride back. You may want to bear this fact in mind during your bombproofing training.

If you are tuned in to your horse and really 'listening' to him as you lead or ride him, most times you will notice if he feels afraid of something and you can become aware of his apprehension before he reacts. In this way you can prevent a drama turning into a crisis.

Although timid, horses are by nature very inquisitive creatures so, once they start to feel safe enough and interested in exploring the world with us, they really start to enjoy the stimulation of discovering new things.

BASIC RIDING SKILLS

How well schooled is your horse?

Before riding out in the big, wide world, where you and your horse may encounter all manner of frightening objects and situations, it is important that your horse is well schooled in the basic aids.

The aids are the means – 'spoken' via the legs, reins, seat and voice – by which the rider communicates to the horse requests to move forwards, sideways, backwards, turn right or left and to stop. You should not ride out without first training the horse to perform all of these movements obediently, softly and without hesitation. Of course, once the horse can happily do all this in a quiet place like a riding arena, he will have to be taken out and about and gradually taught to be as responsive to you, his rider, in the outside world, where there are many more distractions.

It is particularly useful to have a horse that will (a) move sideways away from your leg, and (b) bend his head to the left or right easily and without resistance.

How well schooled are YOU?

It is all very well having a well-schooled horse, but the rider also plays an important part in the bombproofing process. If the rider is very nervous the horse will pick up the rider's fear and become afraid too; so it is important that the rider develops a calm attitude within, in order to help the horse to feel safe.

Before taking a horse out into potentially unpredictable situations, the rider needs to have a good command of his or her own body and be able to give the aids in an appropriate and correct way.

The rider should sit softly and with balance, rather than gripping with the legs or clutching the reins, especially when the horse is frightened, as doing so would make the horse feel more upset. If the rider can stay relaxed, talk soothingly and stroke the horse's neck when it is afraid, so much the better.

It is also important that the rider and the horse are a good match for each other: e.g. it is no good having a novice rider on a challenging and over-lively horse. Riders must be honest about their ability and ride only horses that they can comfortably cope with and at a level that is suitable for their standard of riding. A horse that is too much for the rider or makes the rider feel nervous, puts the rider in danger and may also upset the horse. Even a bombproof horse can become quite nervous if repeatedly ridden by a very anxious rider.

Remember that in order to train your horse to be bombproof, you have to stay calm at all times and avoid getting angry, impatient or tense. In a sense, you have to be bombproof yourself!

You should be able to move the horse sideways, away from your leg, obediently and without hesitation.

What equipment do you need?

In order to be safe you will need good-fitting tack for the horse, a riding hat to current standards, suitable riding boots and gloves. You may also wish to have a neckstrap fitted loosely around the base of the horse's neck for you to hold on to, in case he moves in a quick and unseating way when ridden.

For bombproofing your horse from the ground (leading him past unfamiliar objects) you will need a long lead-line, ideally 12 feet (3.5m) long, and a good halter.

If you are to ride in traffic, wearing bright reflective clothing (for both you and the horse) is a sensible option, so that you can be seen easily by motorists.

As it is best to begin by training your horse to accept all manner of objects in a controlled environment such as a riding arena, you may also want to have a selection of props to hand, such as road cones, sheets of plastic, umbrellas, bicycles – or anything else you can think of that may train him to be bombproof.

It is important that your horse will yield his head softly to both left and right.

An anxious rider can make a horse more nervous; a calm rider can give a horse more confidence.

LEADING SKILLS

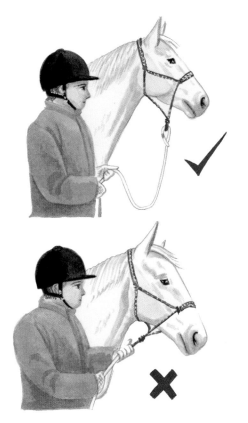

Try to lead the horse with some slack in the rope, rather than holding the horse tightly under the chin.

It is important that you can lead your horse equally well from the left and from the right.

As well as schooling the horse to the riding aids, as part of training a horse to be bombproof it is essential to teach the horse to lead well from the ground.

Assuming your horse leads very well, there can be a number of advantages to leading him in certain situations. Because horses feel safer in groups, being on the ground near your horse's head can give him courage. Seeing you on the ground beside him means that it is not just him who has to push his nose out in front towards the danger.

In some circumstances you may want to place yourself between your horse and the object of his fear, thus getting him used to seeing, hearing or smelling the object and knowing that you are shielding him from it.

The essential point about good leading is to lead your horse with some slack in the rope. If you habitually lead with the rope taut or with a constant contact, your horse will most likely become strong to lead because you already have a lot of pressure on the rope. If you lead him with a little slack in the rope, anytime he goes ahead, behind or moves away sideways, you can correct him with a brief moment or two of contact, which he will be more likely to notice.

To teach your horse to stop well when leading, walk with a little slack in the rope, stop walking, hold the rope in your hand but don't tug it, wait for him to feel the tug he creates and allow him to release the pressure himself.

Remember that for the purposes of bombproofing, it is important that you routinely train your horse to lead equally well from both sides, left and right, so that whichever side a gremlin appears on, you and he will be flexible enough to lead from the better side.

When you practise leading your horse at home or in an arena, see if you can lead him with you at his head, his shoulder or at the girth, depending on what you choose.

Remember that he should move off when you do, stop when you do, and stay out of your body space.

You should endeavour to teach your horse to respect your space whenever you are leading him; this is especially important when he is scared, since it is then that he will instinctively want to bunch up close to you for protection. If you make it a good habit never to allow him to take up your body space, then he will know that it is not something he is allowed to do, even when he is scared.

When leading, walk between the horse and the source of his fear.

It is important that the horse learns to stay out of your personal space.

Avoid leading in a position where the horse might jump into you to avoid a 'monster'.

HOW TO DE-SENSITISE YOUR HORSE

It is possible to get horses used to just about anything: this can be done by a process called 'de-sensitising'. If a horse is exposed to something he finds scary and is given the time to realise that it is not harming him, he will begin to accept it or even totally ignore it. You may have seen examples of this – for example when a new object, such as a sheet of polythene, turns up in the horses' paddock they all run away from it as though it were a monster. If the object is still there after a couple of days, the horses will have accepted it; in fact, they will probably be grazing near it as though it wasn't even there. We can use this same process to de-sensitise our horse: we expose him to whatever is scary to him, and give him all the time he needs to realise that it is not dangerous.

In order to bombproof your horse, to teach him to be braver, less reactive and to trust you more, it is a good idea to have de-sensitising sessions in the school. Put time aside in a safe, controlled environment where you can expose your horse to fearful objects and situations in a gentle and sympathetic way, de-sensitising him slowly, and getting to know what scares him and learning how he is likely to react.

Some of the key elements to de-sensitising a horse are to:

- use distance,
- repeat exposure,
- positive association, and
- start small.

Use distance: For every fearful object, there will be a distance at which the horse feels safe. For example, a horse may be very anxious about a plastic bag that is 4 feet away, but may not worry at all if the same bag is 400 feet away. To de-sensitise the horse, start at a distance where he feels safe and gradually decrease the distance, all the while giving him time to accept the object at each shorter

Use distance to make your horse feel safe, gradually reducing the distance as he becomes more relaxed.

With time and patience, horses will accept all kinds of things without worrying at all.

distance before coming closer. There is no formula for how long this will take: let the horse tell you how long he needs and be infinitely patient. You can tell if he feels unsafe by his actions and tension in his body, and you can tell if he feels safe about something by how relaxed he is.

Repeat exposure: Horses are mostly suspicious of anything new, so it follows that once they have been exposed to something many times, its fear-factor will be reduced. Take the time to expose the horse repeatedly to things in a safe and non-threatening way until he looks quite bored by them!

Positive association: If you can find a way for the horse to associate something positive with the object of his fear, he will accept it much more quickly. For example, if he is afraid of tractors, you may decide to feed him from the back of a tractor until he gets so keen on tractors he will run towards them rather than away! If you want to make him comfortable about something that you can pick up, such as an umbrella, whip, road cone or plastic bag, work slowly with him from the ground until you can stroke him gently with the actual object in such a way that it is pleasurable for him. Remember to stroke him in a regular rhythm and in a way that he will enjoy.

Start small: In a similar way to using distance to reduce the fear-factor, making things smaller can also help the horse. This can apply to something such as a plastic bag, which you can screw up small to begin with, or to something like crossing water, where it may be best to begin with a small puddle and move up to crossing a river.

Get horses used to things by using positive reinforcement: e.g. horse being fed from tractor.

Start small and increase the size of challenges as the horse accepts things.

RIDING PAST OBJECTS OF FEAR

When you ride or lead horses, it is important that you try to see the world through the their eyes, which means noticing the things that horses may find scary. That doesn't mean you ride along getting all tense and looking for things to become nervous about, but it does mean that you should be aware that the horse may react to something and that you are ready to take preventative action.

If you watch a horse as he spots something and shies at it, normally he will look at the object with his head turned towards it, then jump away in the opposite direction. However, it is harder for him to react this way and easier for you to control him, if you can turn his head **away** from the object and ask him to 'give' to the leg on the opposite side to the object.

Now you can see how essential it is to have the horse's basic schooling well established. In particular he must be obedient to the aids, especially when it comes to moving away from the leg, riding in the shoulder-in position or, at the very least, turning the horse's head softly and easily to the right and left. (In the shoulder-in the horse moves sideways and forwards at the same time, with his body and head bent away from the direction he is going – see illustration opposite.)

As you approach an object that may be a problem, and before the horse has reacted to it, get his attention by asking him to yield his head slightly to the opposite rein and to respond to your leg (ideally the leg on the side opposite the object); or put him into a shoulder-in position, with his head turned away from the object and his hindquarters turned towards it. In many cases this is enough to get your horse past without any bother. If you can do this without making an 'issue' out of it, then the horse's flight instincts will be unlikely to surface.

If the horse does react to something he sees, avoid kicking him, pulling him about with the reins, shouting, bullying or getting angry, as this may upset the horse and prove to him that there is something to be scared of – you! Kicking and getting too involved will also bring more energy to the situation and that increased energy may back-fire on you, meaning that if he does react, he will probably react with more effort: that could mean leaping sideways further, rearing higher, spinning faster or bolting for home like lighting.

It is better to follow the procedure described above: make sure that you remain fully seated in the saddle and are looking at the horizon, in the direction you want to go,

Avoid making a big issue out of something.

Look straight ahead past the object, turn the horse's head and body slightly away from the object, or put him into shoulder-in, and walk him past.

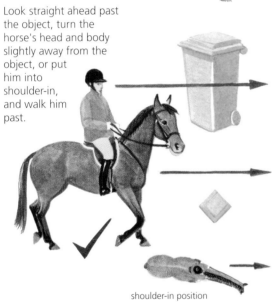

shoulder-in position

pull, pull

kick, kick

Avoid kicking, shouting or whipping him past objects as that may make him feel more threatened. Instead give him time to stand and look, but don't allow him to turn around and run off the other way.

rather than at the object the horse is afraid of. Be totally committed, calm, firm and very patient.

If the horse tries to turn around and run the other way, use one rein or the other to turn him back to face the way you want to go. Do this as many times as you need to, but always effectively and smoothly.

If, after you have given him plenty of time to have a look, the horse 'freezes up' (his feet are stuck to the ground and he just won't go forwards), you can often get him moving again by turning him in small circles. Start turning him with one rein and both legs, using the movement around the circles to get him going forward again.

If the horse is becoming a problem to ride and you have trained him to lead well, it may sometimes help to dismount quietly and lead him past the object, making sure you walk between the horse and the source of his fear. Once past, quietly remount and continue on as though nothing has happened.

Remember that one of the keys to bombproofing your horse is to ensure that every time you go past fearful objects, the outcome is a positive one for you and the horse: that way, he gains in courage and his trust in you grows.

TRAFFIC, TRACTORS, BIKES, HORSES AND CARTS, ETC.

Don't take horses out on busy roads until they have been trained and are accustomed to the sights and sounds of traffic.

It is a good idea to turn horses out in pasture next to a road, where they can see traffic and become de-sensitised to it naturally.

Riding horses in traffic can be quite dangerous but is sometimes unavoidable. Even if your horse is good in traffic, that does not take account of what the other road-users might do, nor of if your horse takes fright at something in the hedgerow when you are adjacent to traffic.

Before riding in traffic, make sure you understand the Highway Code, you and your horse are correctly kitted out and ideally you have reflectors on yourself and even on your horse.

It is not OK to get a horse used to traffic by suddenly riding out along a main road or busy street. If possible, arrange to have the horse turned out in a field beside a road, so that the passing traffic will de-sensitise him every day. Alternatively, take the horse to a quiet spot where there is room for him to move safely out of the way and where there is only a small amount of slow traffic. Make sure that there is enough space so that he can stand some way away from the actual vehicles until he relaxes. As he becomes more used to the traffic at a distance, gradually take him nearer and nearer to it.

Because horses are herd animals, it can be a good idea to ride out in traffic with a schoolmaster horse that is totally traffic-proof. The schoolmaster can be positioned between the new horse and the traffic, and set an example of calmness, showing that it is fine to be among traffic.

With vehicles such as motorbikes and bicycles, it is helpful to de-sensitise your horse in an arena. Ask a friend to ride around him at a distance at which he feels safe, gradually decreasing the distance as the horse becomes more relaxed. Alternatively, to begin with, you can get the friend to sit on the bike in the centre and ride the horse in a circle around the bike. It is a good idea to use this method to get the horse used to being approached from behind as well as from the front.

One thing that seems to build the horse's confidence is if he follows the object of his fear as it moves away from him: doing this can give the horse a sense of courage that he wouldn't have if the object were coming towards him.

Remember that horses leap away from the direction that they are looking with their heads, so if you are alongside traffic and the horse shies at something in the hedgerow, it may be best turn his head towards the traffic, so that it is more difficult for him to jump into the traffic.

As with anything, horses get used to traffic the more they are exposed to it and have positive experiences.

Interestingly, ridden horses can become quite afraid of horses and carts, perhaps because of the strange sight and also because of the noise. Follow the procedures above to get your horse used them.

Turn the horse's head towards the traffic – if there is something scary in the hedgerow, this makes him less likely to jump into the traffic.

To get a horse used to bicycles, in a safe place have a friend ride around the horse, and the horse go around the bicycle.

LOUD NOISES AND UNUSUAL SOUNDS

Use distance to make the horse feel safe, keep repeating the sound and gradually bring the horse nearer, making sure he feels relaxed before each time you move him closer.

Horses have very sensitive hearing and can be upset by loud or unusual noises, but like most other stimuli, they can become used to just about any noise. In the days when cavalry carried guns, it was customary to teach the horse to accept gunfire. This was done in the same way as you can teach your horse to accept noises now.

As with visible objects that scare them, horses are de-sensitised to noises by being exposed to them repeatedly and from a distance that they feel safe.

If you have taught your horse to lead well, begin by standing between the horse and the source of the noise. That way he will feel safer with you as a barrier, but also it will avoid him running into you. It is important that your body language reflects a calm attitude during the whole proceedings.

If you are training your horse to accept a particular noise and you have control over the source of the noise, begin by repeating the noise in a very regular rhythm: horses are rhythmic creatures, so a regular rhythm lets the horse know when to expect the next bang, hiss or clonk. If possible, it is also a good idea to begin your training by making the noise fairly quiet, gradually increasing the volume as he accepts it.

REWARD AND PUNISHMENT

It can be quite tempting to get annoyed and punish a horse for shying or 'playing up' at things when out riding, but any punishment you give to the horse can make him associate the punishment with whatever it is that he is afraid of. That is why a clever rider does not punish a horse for stopping, turning, shying or being afraid of objects.

People often reward their horse when it finally goes past something of which it is afraid. This may work in some situations if the timing of the reward is impeccable, but it can actually be quite unhelpful in making your horse bombproof. The potential problem with rewarding a horse in this kind of situation is that the horse may think you are rewarding him for shying, for pointing out the monsters to you, for drawing your attention to them and for going past them with his legs feeling like jelly and his eyes out on stalks!

Consider what happens in the wild. In a herd of horses a confident herd leader will simply pass by an unusual object, while younger horses might pause and show fear before they follow. The herd leader doesn't reward them when they finally run past the object and catch up; he or she just carries on as though nothing happened.

If we reward or punish the horse when it has shown fear and then gone past something, we are being drawn into the horse's drama and giving our energy and attention to what the horse is thinking, instead of bringing him back to following our ideas. Perhaps the most effective thing to do is to copy what herd-leaders do, and that is to deal with the situation without reward or punishment and then carry on as before.

It is not necessarily a good idea to reward a horse as it passes something it finds scary; it may be better to ride on as though nothing happened.

RIDING OVER OBJECTS ON THE GROUND

Sometimes it helps to dismount and show the horse it is safe by walking through or over the 'hazard' yourself.

Because the horse's natural means of survival is to run away, he is instinctively concerned about looking after his feet and legs and keeping a close check on what is on the ground. Hence things like different patches of ground-cover, drains, road-markings, bridges, rivers, ponds, etc. are a potential hazard to him.

If you are having difficulty getting a horse to walk over, across or through something on the ground, first try leading him across. (Be sure to look behind you to check he doesn't make a flying leap and land on you!) Remember to give him as much time as he needs, to have a look and sniff the ground in front of him. Another approach is to use his herd instinct by getting him to follow another horse.

If you are riding and he tries to turn away, use one rein to bring him back around so that he is facing the object you want to cross.

You may find it helpful to set up a lesson in the school, perhaps using a large sheet of plastic and teaching him to walk over it calmly.

With a horse that is not good about crossing water, start out by walking him through small shallow patches of water, such as puddles, or shallow streams with slow current and good, safe crossing places, before getting him to ford rivers or deeper, murky ponds.

Once he has gone over, across or through an object on the ground, as part of his training you may want to turn him around and take him over, across or through it a few times until he accepts it as being totally fine. That way the lesson will sink in; whereas if he goes through only once, he may think his survival was just a stroke of luck and be just as suspicious again next time.

Whenever you ask a horse to walk on or in something, it is essential that it does not harm him – if he decides to trust you and then he gets hurt, he may quite rightly not trust you next time.

It is important to realise that horses cannot see very well in front of them and they don't have the same depth perception as we do. This is because their eyes are on the sides of their head. You can now appreciate that whenever a horse suddenly twists his head sideways and shoots backwards, it is so that he can get a better focus on what is at ground level.

STEP-BY-STEP TIPS FOR GOING ACROSS OBJECTS ON THE GROUND

You can get a horse to trust you about walking over all sorts of obstacles on the ground by having training sessions somewhere safe, such as a school, and using a prop such as a sheet of polythene or a rubber mat.

STEP 1: Begin by making your prop as small as possible and quietly lead your horse over the object, with you walking casually across it first.

STEP 2: If the horse hesitates, avoid putting him under pressure, just give him time to look, have a sniff and make his mind up that it is safe: continue to be committed to him crossing, until he does.

STEP 3: Once the horse has crossed it for the first time, give him half a minute to relax and then ask him to do the same again back the other way. Gradually encouraging him to go across before you, or even while you stay on the other side.

STEP 4: Once he is totally unphased by going across the object, make it a little larger and repeat the same process. Continue to make the object larger and repeat the process until he will walk calmly across when it is fully unfolded, eventually asking him to pause and stand calmly on it. When he is willing to remain standing on the object with all four feet, you will know that he is totally comfortable with it!

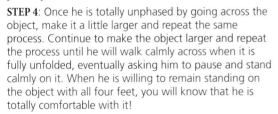

STEP 5: When you and the horse are ready, mount him and ride him across the object, asking him to pause and stay on it for a few moments. When he is standing on the object in a relaxed way, let him stay there a while and stroke his neck.

ANIMALS AND CHILDREN

However much control you may have over your horse, it is not possible to control other animals or people when you are out riding.

Small children, in particular, can be very lively, running about, shouting and not realising that they are upsetting a horse.

Horses are commonly said to be afraid of pigs and donkeys, but some horses can take fright if dogs suddenly jump out and bark. Ridden horses can also be startled by cattle or loose horses in a field, a sheep having a good scratch, or even by a domestic cat that skulks across the path in front of it.

Once you are out riding you cannot control any of these living obstacles, so really it is a good idea to expose your horse to them as much as possible in a safe and gradual way before going out into the world.

To get your horse used to children, it may be a good idea to let your horse see any children that visit the stable yard and allow him to become used to their quick movements and loud voices. Remember that whenever small children are around your horse you need to be vigilant and keep the horse where it will not be able to knock them over. It can help to tie your horse up outside his stable and have children groom him and stroke him: this will be great fun for the children and your horse will be learning

something too.

Horses that share their pasture with other animals will soon accept that they are safe, so wherever possible, see if you can have your horse turned out together with, or next to, other animals. Of course this is not always easy, especially if you want to get your horse used to pigs.

If you know the whereabouts of pigs in your area, it may be as well to take your horse for bombproofing sessions near to the pigs. If your horse is good to lead, work with him from the ground, starting at a safe distance from the pigs and at which he is comfortable to begin, gradually getting nearer to them as he becomes more relaxed. When he is totally comfortable near the pigs with you standing on the ground, it is time to take him a safe distance away and repeat the procedure with you in the saddle.

Remember that a horse is usually more afraid of an animal if it is coming towards him, as his natural prey instinct tells him to run because he may be eaten. Horses are less afraid of something if it is moving away from them, so it can be an advantage to move boldly towards cattle and make them move away from your horse, rather than let them follow him, crowd him or make him think he is being chased.

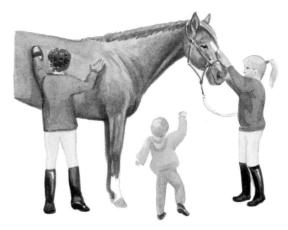

Having children groom and be around your horse in the stable yard is a good way to get him used to their loud voices and quick movements.

If you want to get your horse to be OK with pigs, take him past them at a distance where he feels safe, and remember to position yourself between the pigs and the horse.

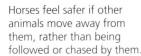

Horses feel safer if other animals move away from them, rather than being followed or chased by them.

'STRANGE' OBJECTS

As far as horses are concerned, the world is full of suspicious and unusual objects of all kinds and colours: road signs, umbrellas, pushchairs, fires, washing on a clothes line, discarded rubbish, etc. In truth, you never know what you might encounter when you ride your horse out into the world, but you can teach him to think before he reacts, and to trust that if you say something is OK, then it probably is.

In some ways, training your horse to be bombproof to strange objects can be one of the easiest and most fun things to set up and do together. Once again, find a safe space to work and, if he is good to lead, begin working with your horse from the ground.

Remember that in all of these situations, because horses are herd animals, he will be acutely aware of your body posture and the mental attitude you have, so set him a good example by making sure your own body language is relaxed and quiet at all times.

The techniques you will most likely use for this are to start by making the object smaller or, if that isn't possible, make it more distant to begin with, and ideally make the horse's experience a positive one. We will use a plastic carrier bag as a tool in the step-by-step guide opposite, but if it is something too big to pick up or you cannot make it smaller, such as a pushchair, begin by standing between the object and the horse: or you could try putting the horse's feed near to the object on a regular basis to create a positive association for the horse.

In a safe situation, there are so many objects and props that you can collect and play with around your horse to help get him used to the outside world. You can stroke him with your riding whip, flapping bags or road cones; play music or ring bells; or play with empty feed bags or refuse bags filled with tin cans – the possibilities are endless. Use your imagination and all the while carry on getting your horse used to as many fun things as possible.

STEP-BY-STEP GUIDE TO DECREASING FEAR OF FLAPPING OBJECTS

When out riding you may encounter all manner of objects that flap or rustle. A useful way to train your horse to be less affected by these things is to set up training sessions somewhere safe using a carrier bag, as shown below.

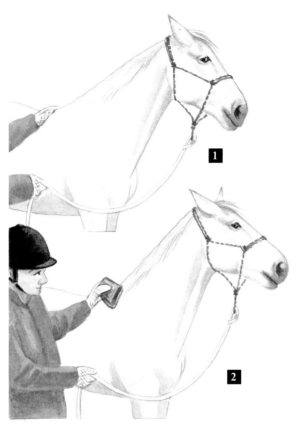

STEP 1: Working your horse from the ground, stroke your horse with your hand so that he becomes really relaxed. It would be ideal if you could stroke your horse all over – left, right, his neck, body, hindquarters and head, maybe even his legs.

STEP 2: With your back to the horse, quietly screw up the carrier bag, tightly in your hand, then stroke him again all over in the same way as you did with your hand, making it as pleasurable as possible. Make sure you stroke the horse softly and with a very regular rhythm.

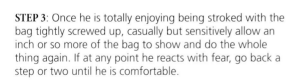

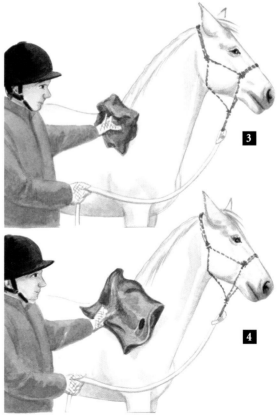

STEP 3: Once he is totally enjoying being stroked with the bag tightly screwed up, casually but sensitively allow an inch or so more of the bag to show and do the whole thing again. If at any point he reacts with fear, go back a step or two until he is comfortable.

STEP 4: Taking your time, allow more and more of the bag to show while having the horse stay calm. You should eventually be able to have the whole bag showing and flapping while you stroke him with it.

CONCLUSION

A horse that is bombproof is a joy to ride. It is lovely to know that your four-legged partner trusts you and accepts that when he is with you he considers the world to be a safe place.

During the course of this book we have looked at some essential principles for teaching horses to become more bombproof – which means that they think more and react less. We have also looked at some common problem areas that can spark off fearful responses in horses.

It is important to realise that horses are instinctively reactive creatures, which means that taking fright at things is part of their nature, and that they should not be punished for this kind of behaviour.

For our part we need to be patient and consistent about introducing them to all manner of objects, obstacles, sights and sounds that they may encounter while being ridden, and we must allow them time to realise that they don't need to be afraid and that being ridden can be an enjoyable, safe and fun experience.

Through being patient and by following these methods, in time you may find that your horse has become the kind of paragon that we traditionally call 'bombproof'.

Happy riding, and may you and your horse be able to trust each other more and more.